For my brothers, Terry, Brad and Darren.
Not only did you provide inspiration for
certain aspects of the brother in this story,
you enjoy pondering life "out there."

"Whatever their bodies do affects their souls."
—C.S. Lewis

Destination
Human

K.L. Denman

Orca currents

ORCA BOOK PUBLISHERS

Library and Archives Canada Cataloguing in Publication

Denman, K. L., 1957-
Destination human / K.L. Denman.
(Orca currents)

Issued also in electronic formats.
ISBN 978-1-4598-0372-5 (bound).--ISBN 978-1-4598-0371-8 (pbk.)

I. Title. II. Series: Orca currents
PS8607.E64D47 2013   jC813'.6   C2013-901872-7

First published in the United States, 2013
Library of Congress Control Number: 2013935296

Summary: An alien inhabits the body of a high-school girl.

*Orca Book Publishers is dedicated to preserving the environment and has
printed this book on Forest Stewardship Council® certified paper.*

Orca Book Publishers gratefully acknowledges the support for its
publishing programs provided by the following agencies: the Government
of Canada through the Canada Book Fund and the Canada Council for the Arts,
and the Province of British Columbia through the BC Arts Council
and the Book Publishing Tax Credit.

Cover photography by Getty Images
Author photo by Jasmine Kovac

ORCA BOOK PUBLISHERS
PO Box 5626, Stn. B
Victoria, BC Canada
V8R 6S4

ORCA BOOK PUBLISHERS
PO Box 468
Custer, WA USA
98240-0468

www.orcabook.com
Printed and bound in Canada.

16 15 14 13 • 4 3 2 1

Chapter One

For Universals like me, traveling between dimensions should be easy. We simply think about where we want to go, and we're there. The key word is *want*. Because of that one word, I'm having trouble getting to the human dimension. My thinking is muddled. It goes something like this: "Destination, Earth—I don't want to do this. Earth.

Earth. Here I go—I *really* don't want to do this."

Professor Float notices my difficulty. "Welkin, do you want to repeat my class yet again?"

"No."

"Then," Float says, "you really *do* want to go to Earth. Remember, you must remain with your host a mere three days of Earth time."

"Um," I mumble, "how long is that again?"

Float's tone is impatient. "Roughly the same span of time as one bioethics class."

"Right." I don't say that that sounds way too long.

"Do you remember all the instructions?" Float asks.

Do I? I think back on the past few classes we've spent preparing for this journey. They might equal two weeks of Earth time, but it wasn't enough for me. Bioethics is hard. I prefer math, because it's orderly. Or history, since what happened in the past is known, and surprises are unlikely. Bioethics includes history, but there is so much more. Experiments are expected. Theories must be formed. We must ponder life and morality, subjects I find highly uncertain.

I think about the day Professor Float announced this final project. Float had dropped hints about it all term. We were warned that our final project would be a challenge that made up 50 percent of our final grade. Sadly for me, Float's tone is so dull and flat, it often puts me into doze mode. I was dozing before the announcement that day.

I do recall Float saying, "Life exists in many forms. In ancient times, it was believed that the two categories of life were plant and animal. We, of course, know better. We know that the proper categories of life are physical and nonphysical."

That was simple enough. Basic history.

Float droned on. "For your final project, you can choose from one of three assignments. Basically, you can focus on the past, the present or the future."

"We can do our project on the past?" I asked.

"Indeed." Float's tone actually rose. "You could conduct a study of primitive life."

"Sign me up for that one," I said.

Float focused on me. "Ah. Welkin. I haven't explained the specifics. That assignment is the most difficult."

Snickers arose from my classmates. I refused to back down. "I am interested in the past," I said firmly.

"Very well. I've made a note of your choice." Float paused before asking, "Would you like to hear the details?"

"Yes." I imagined visiting the Thought Archives and quietly browsing old files.

I would then present an excellent report for which I would receive top marks.

"Perhaps this will be good for you, Welkin," Float muttered. "Your project will begin with your entry into a physical host. The host will be a juvenile human on the planet Earth. This will enable you to experience a physical form similar to that of our ancestors. While you inhabit this host, you will collect data for a full report on the nature of life in that form."

I went completely blank.

"Do you understand, Welkin?"

My response was something like, "Gah."

"I'll take that as a yes." And then Float had gone on to describe the other assignment options. I'd been too stunned to absorb a single word—

"Welkin!" Float's voice jars me back to the present.

"Yes?"

Float is annoyed. "I asked if you remembered all the instructions."

"I do." I hope that's true.

"Then go."

"*Destination, Earth,*" I think.

And I'm there.

Almost at once, I sense that earthlings are indeed thinking beings. Thoughts abound. But it's impossible to understand anything. It's all gibberish.

"Nothing but primitives," I tell myself. What can I possibly learn here that I couldn't access in the Thought Archives? Isn't downloading a description of an experience just as good as experiencing one?

Wait. My earlier research showed that humans aren't the only sentient species on Earth. So some of the thoughts I hear may not be human. Also, humans communicate in different languages. How bizarre is that, a species whose members can't communicate with each other? Float has made me learn a language known as English. I'm supposed to scan the planet until I locate thoughts in English words. That turns out to be easy enough.

The next task is trickier. I must locate the juveniles. Humans tend to gather in groups according to their age. They have special structures for juveniles, known as schools. The juveniles are herded into these schools for education. I was surprised to learn of that, because it sounds familiar.

Float had explained a key difference. "Human schools are limited by physical form. Juvenile humans have other gathering places, such as malls and stadiums. When seeking them, listen for a tremendous focus on their bodies. Thoughts about appearance, food and mating will be very prominent."

I don't understand what Float had described. I studied it but could not relate to any of it. For now, first things first. I must find the juveniles.

It doesn't take long. Just as Float said, I find a mass of humans clamoring with thoughts about their physical form. It's astonishing! I hear bits of thought from hundreds of minds. *So hungry. Bad hair. My butt's too big. Does he think I'm cute?*

Thought after thought is focused on their physical life. *That stinks. Horrible cramps. Such gorgeous eyes. Does she think I'm hot?*

It's overwhelming. I know some of these thoughts relate to the sensory organs, and, in theory, I understand the five senses. But "he" and "she" are confusing. What is a he or a she? I accessed files on that topic, too, but they didn't make sense. I can't recall the specifics, but it seems like this might be a big deal among humans. So how am I supposed to choose the right one?

As far as I can tell, the humans are virtually the same. I decide to go with a random selection. I believe that's a scientific approach. No bias and all that. I prepare myself for entry and then recall that the best moment for me to take control of the host is during its sleep cycle. That's similar to doze mode. So I zero in on a particular juvenile and follow it from the school.

This human transports itself to a nearby location. It tends to its bodily functions and thinks numerous baffling thoughts. Finally, it enters a rest period. I recognize this by the human's lack of conscious thought.

My moment has come. Float instructed me on the optimum method of entry. "Enter the host through an existing portal. I recommend the mouth or the nostril. When the body inhales air, you can be absorbed along with it."

Air is a mixture of elements. On Earth, the air element required by animal life is oxygen. I am not oxygen, but I can blend with it. I position myself near the human's nostril and await inhalation.

And things go terribly wrong.

Another life form interferes. This being is a parasite that I believe is called a mosquito. As I align myself to become one with the human, I accidentally enter the mosquito.

The mosquito is a single-minded creature with an objective similar to mine. It enters the host, but not through air. No, it punctures the skin organ and proceeds to download a substance known as blood. This unexpected turn of events is what I despise about experiments.

No matter. I move through the mosquito. All bodies occupied by Universals die when we depart. So as I leave the mosquito behind, its body dies. And just like that, I am inside the human.

AGGGH!

My mind explodes. The rush of sensation is dazzling. Bewildering. Nothing could have prepared me for the enormity of this moment. There is too much incoming data all at once. I fear my thoughts will be permanently scrambled—I'll go insane.

I order myself to *think,* but I have no words for the things I'm experiencing. I'll have to get out. Escape. Flee. Run.

Run. That's a *physical* word! I'm already thinking like a human! I cling to this hope as my being spreads through the host body, filling it like air inside a balloon. I find the body's outer limits and hold myself there. The skin organ is basically a containment bag. While I dislike being imprisoned by it, that is the assignment. Stay inside the host.

I recall something else about the skin. It's a dangerous method of entry.

Chapter Two

"Eeeeeee!"

What *is* that?

"Omigod, omigod, omiGAAAWD! What's happening to me?"

My host is speaking. I don't believe this should occur.

It says, "It shouldn't. This is wrong. All wrong!"

Very wrong.

"Wait," it squawks. "I must be having a nightmare."

A nightmare? Oh, yes. A form of sleep disturbance.

"Only it seems like it's still happening." My host sounds puzzled. "I'm awake now. Helloooo."

Is it greeting me?

It shouldn't be able to talk, but it keeps going. "Whoa! Maybe this is one of those lucid dreams Madison was talking about."

A lucid dream?

"Yeah." It expels a gust of air. "So all I have to do is go back to sleep, and this will stop."

I certainly hope so.

"Me too," it mumbles. And I sense its consciousness fading.

I focus hard on absolutely nothing. It's a technique Universals learn so that they can cloak their minds from other Universals. I'm not very good at it.

But I believe I manage to hide my presence from the human while it returns to sleep.

And then I let myself panic over the problem with skin. Float said entry via skin is risky. Something to do with triggering the host body's immune system? No, that wasn't it. I didn't pay close attention because I knew I'd take the safest route, through a nostril. Until I didn't. Horrid mosquito!

I recall that skin entry isn't a fatal error. Does it prevent me from suppressing the host? That could be it. Ideally, the host is entered during doze mode and is unaware that it has been occupied. It should remain dozing while I have control of the body.

I suspect I have a problem. But, really, how bad can it be? I am the superior intelligence here. That will allow me to control the human when it wakes. If it wakes. It might not. Now that it's sleeping again, it could simply carry on doing that.

Or not. In which case, my best strategy is to master the operation of the body. I am most interested in the sensory organs. For example, the nose. It detects odors in the air. It is connected to the breathing apparatus. Lungs? Yes. They are supposed to be self-regulating. I locate them, and, sure enough, they are automatically expanding and contracting. Amazing.

I check out a few more internal organs. The heart is pumping blood. The stomach is digesting food. The liver is filtering blood. My host appears to have an excellent body.

Back to the nose. I attempt sniffing and find a variety of smells. I don't know what they indicate, but they are there. Another sensing feature is the ear. There are two of them, and with these I should hear sound. And I do. I hear the movement of breath. And something else. It's a persistent sound emanating from outside the body. Is it possible someone is attempting to communicate with my host?

It's another shrill "eeeeeee" sound. I attempt to listen for thoughts from the "eeeeeee" being but hear nothing. Then I recall a sickening detail. It is extremely rare for humans to hear the thoughts of other beings. Possibly, the skin bag blocks this. They must rely on their physical senses to perceive everything.

That is truly primitive. And I, too, will be stuck with this handicap for an entire bioethics class. Float is a cruel teacher.

So how can I figure out what is making that sound? Oh yes. I should use the eyes. I locate them in the head where they should be, but they seem to be malfunctioning. I can't see a thing. Then a point on my skin bag produces a sensation. Skin is the sensory organ that provides touch data. This touch is unpleasant. In fact, I believe it is the sensation known as pain.

My host emits a muffled moan (a very bad sign), and quite suddenly, one of our limbs jerks into motion and swings about. "Stupid mosquito," my host mutters. Then our eyes begin functioning. I perceive dim light and the form of another mosquito dodging the limb.

And then, "What IS this?" My host is talking again. "Who ARE you? WHAT are you? WHAT ARE YOU DOING IN MY HEAD?"

"That's a lot of questions," I say.

"Oh. My. God!" my host screeches. "Get OUT!"

Carefully, I say, "I can't do that yet."

It propels our body upright, which is a dizzying sensation. It then proceeds to strike our head with our hand. I experience pain again and dislike it. "Stop that," I say.

"Leave! Now!" It continues hitting us.

Perhaps my host isn't so excellent. "Are you defective?" I ask it. "You're hurting us."

"Us? *Us*?" it asks. "There is no US! Get out!"

"I told you I can't do that," I say. "It would mean an automatic fail for me. The proper thing for you to do is to simply obey me. I'm in charge now."

It stops hitting us and collapses our body downward. "Ahhhhh!" it moans. "I've lost my mind."

"Not exactly," I tell it. "You're simply hosting me for a short time. Three days, by your calendar. Nothing is required of you other than your body."

"And you think *I'm* defective?" it asks. "Who are you?"

"My name is Welkin. I'm a Universal. You are a juvenile human."

"I thought I was dreaming," it mutters. "But no. I've lost it. Totally lost it."

"What did you lose?" I ask.

"My mind, you idiot!" it shrieks. "What do you think?"

"I think many things."

"Yeah. I can tell," it says. "Like, totally rude stuff."

"I beg your pardon?"

"For one thing, you think of me as an *it*. I am not an *it*. And who says stuff like 'juvenile human'? That's creepy." It pauses, then asks, "Are you some sort of perv?"

"I'm not familiar with that term. I already told you, I'm a Universal. I'm a superior nonphysical being, and I'm here to study you."

"You are *sooo* a perv!" it says. "And my name is Chloe. Got that, Welkin? That's not too hard for you, is it?"

I can't believe this. It—that is, *Chloe*— is implying that I lack intelligence.

"Too right, Welkin. That's exactly what I'm saying. You know why? Because any freaky blob creature who thinks he can just hang out in *someone else's* body"—Chloe pauses to draw breath—"is a total moron."

I know this word, *moron*. It is not flattering. "Chloe, that's enough. Calm yourself. Try to be rational. Most preferably, go back to sleep for three days."

Abruptly, it sits up and swings our legs off the bed. "I'm telling my mother," it says.

Mother? "Ah, yes. That would be your parent, correct? What are you going to tell it?"

Chloe doesn't answer immediately, and it's then that I realize I can't hear its thoughts. But obviously, it can hear mine. Such as my thinking of it as "it." How can that possibly be rude? I concentrate fiercely on hearing its thoughts and get nothing. This is very bad.

"Aha! So that's how it is, eh?" Chloe crows. "Looks like Mr. Superior Welkin isn't so superior after all."

"You should go talk to your mother," I say.

"Why?" Its tone is suspicious.

I attempt to cloak my mind as I think how the mother human might agree that Chloe has lost her mind. If the information in the Thought Archives is correct, the mother would then take Chloe to a doctor. This doctor would likely drug Chloe, and then I—

"Welkin! That's evil! You want me drugged?"

So much for the mind cloak. "This is a disaster," I say.

"Too right," it says. "So you'll leave now?"

"Absolutely not," I tell it. "If you refuse to sleep, then we'll have to find a way to co-exist."

"That is so *not* happening." Chloe shakes our head rapidly from side to side, and our field of vision blurs.

"Why not?" I ask.

Chloe snorts. "Why not? The better question is, why would I? This is *my* body, and you're trespassing. You didn't even ask. You barged in and—oh, forget it. I don't have to explain. Just *go*!"

"That is an excellent question," I say.

"Huh?"

"Your question about why you would agree to co-exist with me," I explain. "I'd like to answer that question."

"Welkin, I don't need you to—"

"No, it's quite all right," I interrupt. "I *want* to answer. My answer is that you'd agree because it would provide you with the opportunity to study *me*. You see?"

"Wow. That is *so* lame. Do you honestly think I've ever given a single thought to studying a Unitard?"

"Universal," I correct. "I'm a Universal."

"Whatever," it sighs. "Give it up, Welkin."

It appears that I am unable to suppress my host. Nor will it cooperate. Conclusion—Chloe is correct, and my only option is to give up. This means I'll have to take Float's dreadful bioethics class yet again. Thinking about another eon of that droning voice is deeply depressing. And then there will be the cruel mockery of my classmates…that will be the worst.

Chapter Three

"Aw, Welkin, really?" Chloe asks. "The other Unis will laugh at you?" It shakes our head again, slowly this time.

I can't answer it. I can only think about how dismal it is to be a failure.

"Listen…" Chloe murmurs. Then she quickly adds, "No, forget it. I really shouldn't." She pauses again as she drums our fingers on a nearby table.

"But then," she goes on, "it's only for three days, right? It would be sort of like having a pet, wouldn't it? Although I'd prefer a kitten to an alien."

"What are you saying?" I ask.

"Well. If you could stop thinking of me as an *it*—females are *her* or *she*— I might be willing to help you out."

"You'd help me? Allow me to stay and experience the physical form?" This is amazing behavior for a primitive.

"I'm *not* a primitive, Welkin," Chloe says. "Man, you have a *lot* to learn."

"I do," I tell it. Her. "Such as, what is a female? And can you hear everyone's thoughts or only mine? And what is a perv?"

"Wow. This is going to be harder than I thought." Chloe scratches our head. It feels pleasant. "I think we need some rules."

"Okay." I attempt to operate the limb that scratches our head.

"That's rule one right there," Chloe says. "*I'm* in charge of my body. You leave the operating to *me*." She glances at a device that displays symbols, then groans. "Right now, I have to get this body ready for school."

"Is that difficult?" I ask.

"I'll know as soon I look in the mirror." She puts our body in motion and exits the sleeping chamber. She halts quite suddenly at the entrance to another room. "I have to pee," she says.

Her tone suggests this is important, but I don't understand her meaning.

"It means I'd like some privacy," she says. "*Especially* if you're a guy."

This is surprising. I'd begun to think Chloe was intelligent in her own way. But she appears to have forgotten a simple fact. "Chloe," I say, "I'm a Universal."

She sighs heavily. "Duh. I know that, Welkin. But are you a guy Uni or a girl?"

"I don't understand."

"Oh, man. You must be one or the other. You know, male or female? Like, when you're in your own body, do you, um…" She hesitates, then blurts, "Do you stand or sit to use the toilet?"

Toilet. In English, a receptacle for bodily wastes.

"No kidding." Her tone is sarcastic.

I'm aware of an uncomfortable pressure building in our body. "I don't have bodily wastes," I tell her.

"Yeah, right. Even bugs have to go," she says.

"But Chloe, I don't *have* a body. And I must tell you, I believe that something is amiss with ours."

"You *never* had a body?" she asks. "Ever?"

"I am a nonphysical being from another dimension who—"

"Yeah, yeah. Totally weird. I get it." She proceeds toward the toilet. "Don't watch, Welkin," she says.

Don't watch? I can only see what she sees. Chloe reacts to my thought by closing our eyes. Then she sits and discharges liquid waste. Almost at once, the uncomfortable pressure I noticed is relieved.

"How often does this bodily function occur?" I ask.

"I don't know. Too often," Chloe replies. "Lucky you, not having to bother."

I am indeed lucky.

Chloe completes the toilet task and reopens our eyes. She proceeds to a sink, where she washes our hands. Then she views our body in the mirror. "Ahh!" she moans. "My hair! And is that a zit on my nose?"

I observe my human for the first time. Some body parts are covered with clothing, but what is visible appears to be standard. Chloe is currently focused on only two aspects. First, the hair.

She's ignoring the tiny hairs we have all over our skin. Instead, she glares only at the mass on our head. It appears to be growing out of control.

"Very funny, Welkin," she says.

I assume the hair mass on our head is abnormal. It's clearly different from the rest. Possibly some form of medical treatment is required. "Did it sprout overnight?" I ask.

"No. It's supposed to be there. But it got messed up while I was sleeping."

"Hmm," I say. "Will it be difficult to remove?"

"I don't want to *remove* it, Welkin. I have to *fix* it. And this zit!" She leans toward the mirror to study a red spot on her nose. "Strange. Maybe it's not a zit. It's itchy. Oh. Frickin' mosquito bite."

"Quite right," I say.

"Okay, Welkin? I can't talk for a while. I've got a lot to do, and I need to focus."

"Please," I say. "Carry on with your duties."

She doesn't answer. She washes our face. Next, she cleans our teeth with a small brush and a length of string. I enjoy the odor of the paste she uses, but the taste isn't pleasant. After that, the procedure becomes extremely complex.

From a cabinet, Chloe retrieves several items. Two of them are electric-powered. There's also a box filled with various chemicals. She thrusts our head under the tap in the sink and wets our hair mass with water. Then she partially dries the mass with a towel. This is followed by considerable time spent untangling the hairs with a comb.

It's plain to see that the water and comb have subdued the abnormal mass. But, incredibly, Chloe then uses one of the electric devices to blow hot air onto the hair. It soon returns to a dry, billowing state. I feel I should point out an obvious flaw in her process.

"I know what I'm doing, Welkin," she says.

I decide to withhold judgment.

"Good call," she says.

"I thought you couldn't speak during this process," I say.

"Of course I *can*," she tells me. "I just don't want to."

I feel slighted, and she says, "Don't go all emo on me, Welks. I need to focus."

Ah. Perhaps her duties are more difficult than they seem. It's likely too much to expect a primitive to do multiple tasks at the same time.

"Jeez," she mutters. But she carries on. She picks up the other electrical device. It too emits heat, and she applies this directly to the hair mass. Slowly and carefully, she draws the device along sections of hair. Soon the hair is once again subdued.

Chloe further subdues it by binding it at the back of our head with elastic. I can't help thinking she could have avoided most of the prior procedure by doing this in the first place.

"Not the same," she mutters. "The ponytail is so I can do my makeup."

Makeup, it turns out, involves the box of chemicals.

"Some of my stuff is organic mineral." Her tone is defensive. But she doesn't say more as she employs fine motor skills to place substances on our skin. There is great focus on the mosquito bite, and soon it is the same color as our skin. Next, the skin above our eyes is colored, and then the lashes are coated with dark goo. Finally, she colors our lips and then once again releases the hair.

"There," she says, as she studies our reflection in the mirror.

Overall, I can see very little difference. However, I must assume that this is necessary to the health of the human body.

"It's got nothing to do with *that*," Chloe says. "I do it so I look good."

"Look good?" I ask.

"When you *look* good," she says, "then you *feel* good."

"I understand."

"You do not. You shouldn't tell lies, Welkin."

Chapter Four

Chloe's hearing my every thought is most annoying.

"And you don't think *you're* annoying?" she asks. Quickly she adds, "Don't answer that. I'm in a hurry. The only thing I want to know is how do you exist without a body? I was thinking about that the whole time I was getting ready."

So she *can* do more than one task at a time. "Getting ready for what?" I ask.

"I already told you," she says. "School."

This seems ridiculous. I feel that *she* is now lying to *me*. School is about the mind. It has nothing to do with looking—

"Welkin," she cuts in. "Please. Just tell me what you are. Don't you dare just say you're a Universal. I mean, what *is* a Universal? Because so far as I know, *everyone* has a body. Even aliens."

"You know some aliens?" I ask.

"Welkin!" she shrieks. "Focus. What *are* you?"

What am I? "I am a thinking being. I am an evolved being. Therefore, I don't require a body to exist."

"That doesn't make sense," Chloe says. "You must have some sort of... substance."

Ah. Her primitive mind requires physical proof. I can't give her that.

She must know I exist, because she's talking to me. But clearly, this is a difficult concept for her. I think hard about how I might explain the nonphysical in simple terms. Simple enough for her to understand.

"If you're so smart," she says, "why can't you explain? Come on, Welks. It's almost eight and I have to get going. If I'm late again, I'll get detention."

I'm unclear on what detention is, but she's given me an idea. "You know what an eight is, don't you?" I ask.

"Well, duh. It's a number."

"Correct," I say. "And what is that?"

"It's…just a number. That's it."

"Do numbers have a physical form?" I ask.

"Yes. No. I don't know," she says. "Why are we talking about numbers?"

"Because you believe they exist," I tell her. "And they do. But, like me, they don't have a physical form."

"I can write a number eight," she retorts.

"That would simply be a *symbol* for the number eight," I say. "Then there's the concept of time. That too lacks substance and..."

"The time! I've gotta go, Welks."

She dashes us back to her sleeping chamber and rummages through numerous items of clothing. While doing this, she mutters aloud. "These jeans? No, I wore them yesterday. Maybe those? No, they're icky. These? I guess. Which top? The blue one. Yeah. Oh, but not with the light blue jeans..."

Selecting apparel seems highly complicated. I try to guess why. Perhaps some clothing is better for protecting the body? Yes, that must be it. Certain parts of the planet are extremely cold while other places are hot. But does this theory apply to the items Chloe is struggling to choose from?

"Again, Welkin," she says, "it's about how they look. It's about *style*."

Style. I remember this word. But it was one I couldn't understand. Much like art, sport, music and dance. These things don't seem to have a purpose.

"Wow, you've got that wrong," Chloe says. "They're all important. Also, they're fun."

"Fun?"

"You'll see," she says. "Let's go."

Chloe has managed to reclothe our body. She grabs some baggage from the floor and moves us briskly out of the room and along a hall. Then she hurtles us down a flight of stairs, moving so fast, I fear we'll crash.

"Is such speed necessary?" I ask.

"You ain't seen nothin' yet," she replies. We enter an area where the air is filled with aromas, and our stomach reacts. It actually emits a growling sound. I also notice another human seated at a table.

"This must be a kitchen," I say. "The food room."

"Yup," Chloe says.

"Huh?" says the other human.

"Nothing," Chloe responds.

"Who is that?" I ask.

She doesn't answer.

"May I greet this human?" I ask.

Chloe removes us from the kitchen and whispers, "Rule two, Welkin. I can't talk to you when other people are around. They'll think I'm nuts."

Nuts. A form of fruit produced by trees. "I fail to see why they would think..."

"Not *those* nuts!" she hisses. "Let me grab some food, and we're out of here."

"But who is that human?" I ask.

"My brother. He's a pest, and I usually ignore him. So no more talking. Got it?"

"I guess." But I'm unhappy about this situation. As we re-enter the kitchen,

I recall that part of my assignment is to interact with other humans. But with her maintaining control of our body, I can't use our vocal cords.

"Suck it up," she whispers.

"Huh?" says the brother human.

Chloe ignores him. She tosses some food items into her baggage, then grabs a small container from a refrigeration unit. She opens this and spoons some of the contents into our mouth. It tastes *much* better than the toothpaste. "What is that?" I ask.

But she simply shakes our head.

"What's wrong with you?" the brother asks.

Chloe spoons another portion of the soft food into our mouth, looks at the brother and rolls our eyes toward the ceiling. The brother reacts by opening its mouth and sticking out its tongue. I believe that muscle is normally used to produce speech, but it doesn't say anything. Rather, it seems to be displaying its partially chewed food.

Chloe sighs and turns away, and the brother sniggers. I realize that they've communicated without using a single word. Fascinating.

Chloe swiftly eats the remaining soft food, grabs another clothing item from a hook on the wall and puts it on our torso. She picks up her baggage and wiggles her fingers in her brother's direction. We exit via a portal, step away from the building and proceed along a cement path.

"Wow," she says.

I believe she may be referring to the food we ate. "What was that?" I ask.

"Peach yogurt," she replies.

"I enjoyed it," I say. "I think we should have had more."

"No time, Welks. We'll eat more later."

I consider pointing out that our stomach would like more also, but she doesn't give me a chance. She says, "Welkin, is there any way you can, like, tune out while I'm at school?"

"Tune out?" I ask.

"You know. Stop being in my head so I don't hear you? Like, go to sleep or something?"

I think about how often bioethics class puts me into doze mode. "It's possible," I say. "But if I do that, I'll miss studying the other juveniles."

"What about that mind cloak thing?" she asks.

"I'm not very good at it."

"I noticed," she says. "But ignoring you is harder than ignoring Josh."

"What's a josh?" I ask.

"Not what. Who. My brother. The kid in the kitchen? Who, by the way, is a *he*."

"Ah."

"*And*," Chloe says, "in a few minutes, I'll be hooking up with some friends. We walk to school together, and we talk.

I can't be talking to you at the same time. And another thing. This is even *more* important."

"Oh?"

"Absolutely," she says. "In fact, it's *crucial*. See, there's this guy I like, and I think he likes me, so I get sort of nervous around him. But that's bad because I need to play it cool, right? I want to find out if he's going to the dance on Friday."

I'm baffled.

"See, I *knew* you would be. Which means you'll ask a lot of stupid questions, and I'll get mixed up." She sighs and adds, "Sorry. They're not *stupid* questions. They're distracting. Oh. There's Madison."

Chloe waves our hand at the approaching human. "So please, Welkin," she whispers. "Just try to lay low, okay?"

"I'll try," I tell her. "But I can't promise anything."

Chapter Five

I succeed in cloaking my mind! We greet the Madison human and several other juveniles without any difficulty. They emit a constant stream of chatter as we walk to the school. The conversation is so rapid and strange, I find it hard to follow. Much of the talk centers on a Noah human. When I reviewed Earth history, this person was mentioned.

He once built an extremely large boat and filled it with animals.

When we enter the school building, Chloe's group disperses into a jostling crowd of other humans. The din is astonishing. I decide it's a good thing I can't hear their thoughts.

"But I can still hear yours, Welks," Chloe mutters.

"You can?"

She halts at a small metal door, one of many, and releases a locking mechanism. She puts our head partially inside the small compartment and says, "Yeah. But you're sort of muffled. I think I can handle it."

Oh. I suppose muffled is better than nothing.

"It is." She withdraws our head as she places some baggage into the compartment and glances about. The crowd continues to swirl around us, and Chloe pops our head back inside.

"But just so you know, Noah is the guy I like. *Not* the one with the ark."

"There's more than one of them?"

"Oh, brother," she sighs.

"Josh is here?" I ask.

"No! Jeez, I don't have time for—"

"Chloe?" A new human voice interrupts us.

The sudden change in our body is alarming. It's as if an electrical current flashes through every molecule and floods us with heat. Chloe straightens abruptly and turns to face the speaker. "Noah," she says. Her voice flutters with residual electricity.

"Hey. Were you, uh, talking to someone?" Noah asks.

"Oh! Ha ha," she laughs. "No."

That's a lie.

"I mean, I, uh," Chloe stammers. "I was talking to myself."

Noah's mouth moves into a smile curve. "You do that often?"

"Uh, no," she says. "Well, maybe sometimes. Just lately, I guess."

Noah raises a brow. "Problem?" he asks.

Our mouth smiles widely as we shrug. "No, no. Everything's cool. How's it going with you?"

"All good," Noah says. He shifts his weight from one foot to the other. "I was wondering about, uh," He pauses to swallow. "The dance."

Oddly, our lungs stop functioning. Chloe barely has enough breath to say, "Oh?"

"Yeah." Noah nods. "Are you going?"

Our stomach is behaving oddly. Perhaps it's begun the work of digesting the yogurt?

We smile at Noah, but our facial muscles feel as if they're straining. "Yeah," Chloe says.

"Cool." Noah grins back. "So I'll see you there?"

"For sure," Chloe replies. A loud ringing sound occurs, and we startle. "Shoot," Chloe says. "I've gotta go. Dorkan's being a cow about lates." We spin away from Noah, and she quickly slams the door to the compartment. Then we turn back to him and smile once more. "So, uh, later?"

He smiles too. "Later." He walks one way while we go the other.

"Frick!" Chloe mutters. "Yogurt!"

"It's very tasty," I say.

"But I don't want to think about *digestion* when…" Chloe catches the eye of an approaching human and forces a smile. "Hey," she says.

The human replies, "Hey" as she passes by us.

"Grrrr," Chloe rumbles. Softly. "Welks, the mind cloak? *Please*."

I'd forgotten the mind cloak. I work at it while we rush down the hall and into a chamber filled with other humans.

They appear to be in a state of chaos. They are flinging baggage and clothing about the room. Chloe joins in. She removes most of the clothing she put on a short time ago and replaces it with other clothing. Incredibly, she also once again binds her hair with elastic.

"Gym class," she mutters.

"I know, hey?" a human responds. "It sucks."

It sucks? I ponder this. Possibly, some sort of vacuum device is involved?

"Exercise," Chloe groans.

Ah. That would be movement of the body to promote physical wellness. The room is emptying rapidly. As another bell sounds, Chloe is the last one through a door into a much bigger chamber.

A large human watches our approach. It is holding a clipboard wedged against its abdomen as it says, "Glad you could join us, Chloe. Take three laps."

"*Three?*" Chloe squeaks. "But Ms. Dork—*Doran*, I was here on time."

The large human's eyes narrow. They almost disappear into the fleshy face. "Barely," it says. "And your attitude hasn't improved, has it?"

Our muscles stiffen as Chloe mutters, "It's fine."

"Is it?" Ms. Dork-Doran asks. Its body appears to swell. This is a most interesting performance for a human. I recall that a certain amphibian being displays this swelling behavior. Also a fish and some birds, such as one known as a turkey.

Chloe suddenly snorts through our nose.

Ms. Dork-Doran sighs, and the swelling subsides. "You're wasting your talent, Chloe. You need to train *hard*."

Chloe directs our gaze toward a door on the far side of the chamber. "Yes, ma'am," she says.

Ms. Dork-Doran's mouth opens as if it has more to say. Then the mouth closes, and it sighs again. "Go," it says before it turns away.

Chloe moves us swiftly toward the far door. When we pass through, we are outside the building. Gray clouds cover the sky, and an expanse of grass stretches before us. Numerous juveniles are scattered about, performing various movements.

"Turkey," Chloe mutters.

"I believe that's correct," I say.

"So do I." She snorts again as she takes us away from the others. We go through a gate and onto a rubbery surface. It's marked with parallel lines that extend away in both directions. "It's a track," she says.

She begins stretching our legs. "Frickin' three laps. I can't *stand* Dorkan. What a hypocrite. Where does she get off telling me I need to train hard?

She should take a look at herself in the mirror."

"Why should she do that?"

"Because then maybe she'd notice *she's* the one who needs to run." Chloe begins moving us along the track with a bouncing gait. "It's called jogging," she says. Then she adds, "I used to like running until she came along and wrecked it."

"I don't understand."

"Why am I not surprised?" Chloe asks. Before I can answer, she says, "It's like this. I'm pretty good at running. Not great or anything. Just good. I mean, in elementary school, I won all the races. But not anymore. There's too much competition."

"You dislike competition?" I ask.

Chloe increases our speed. "I don't mind competition. It's *losing* I don't like."

I struggle to piece this all together. "So, you don't like running anymore because you dislike losing? This causes you to dislike the Dork-Doran?"

"She thinks if I train more, I can win again. She wants me to make her look good."

I am truly confused now. "Possibly, you could allow her the use of your chemicals and hair devices?" I suggest.

"Not *that* sort of looking good," Chloe replies. "I mean, if I win because I do what she says, then she can take the credit."

"I understand," I say.

"Don't lie, Welks," she says. "Okay, no more talking. I'm going to run now."

Chapter Six

I thought we were running but quickly find I was mistaken. Our stride lengthens, and we hurtle forward. The air rushes past our ears, and our vision to either side blurs. We look only ahead, down the track. Our feet striking the ground create a pattern of repeating sound.

I notice that our heart begins to beat faster, our lungs draw more air, and our skin warms. As we round a bend in the track, we see a few other humans ahead of us. Chloe increases our speed, and seconds later we catch up to them and pass them.

One of them calls out, "You go, girl." Chloe responds by raising a hand. Then we go faster yet. We fly past the gate where we entered and keep going. We're halfway around the track again when a light rain begins to fall, misting us with cooling moisture. It's a startling sensation, but almost at once I realize it feels...wondrous.

I have a sudden urge to laugh, and something strange starts happening to my thoughts. They no longer seem separate from our body. It's almost as if I *am* the body, and it is me. We are a marvelous unit in perfect harmony. The only thing that exists is this moment.

I'd like to keep going like this, but by the time we approach the gate once more, our body is tiring. It's becoming difficult to breathe, and our leg muscles are burning. Still, Chloe doesn't slow down until we pass that point.

I don't notice the Dork-Doran standing alongside the track until it yells, "Excellent time on that lap, Chloe. Your personal best."

Chloe doesn't reply as we move past, but then our mouth smiles. We continue at a jog, and she stays quiet as our breathing and heart rate gradually slow.

"That was a superb physical experience," I tell her. "When can we do it again?"

"It was good, wasn't it?" she murmurs.

"*I* think you should disregard the Dork-Doran dilemma and run all the time."

"I can't run *all* the time, Welks," Chloe says. "But I'd forgotten how good it feels to go hard. That *rush* you get."

Rush. A word that means to hurry. Also, a form of tall grass.

"Also," Chloe laughs, "a type of *thrill*."

"Ah. I understand."

"This time," she says, "I think you do."

"So when can we do it again?" I ask.

She shrugs our shoulders. "I don't know. I have a lot of other things to do, you know."

"Like what?" I hope she doesn't mean the boring task of adjusting the hair mass.

"Omigod." She slows to a walk and puts a hand to our head. "My hair. It's getting soaked."

I shouldn't have thought about the hair. I attempt to distract her by asking, "What does omigod mean?"

"It's an expression. Like saying, 'Oh. My. God.' Only fast."

Ah. God. One of the names for the supreme deity. "So when you say that, you're speaking to your God?"

"Um," Chloe says, "I guess I just say it. It's a habit."

Habit. An acquired behavior pattern regularly followed until it becomes almost involuntary.

"Yeah, that would be it," Chloe says. We are nearing the gate once more, and she scans the grassy area between us and the building. All the other humans, including the Dork-Doran, have departed. The rain is falling harder, and our skin feels chilled.

"Our body is becoming uncomfortable," I say.

"Too right, Welks. We should go in. But since we're already wet..." She sets us jogging again, but we don't go toward the door. Instead, we jog alongside the building until we round a corner. We continue following the building to the next corner, where we find a sheltered area. From there we can observe a large rectangle of grass with tall metal posts at either end. We also find a pack of juvenile humans in bulky garb. They are engaged in battle.

"It's not a battle," Chloe says.

"They're bashing and knocking each other around," I point out.

"It's a game called football. See? They're playing with a ball."

I glimpse the ball as one of the humans throws it into the air. It's deformed.

"It's supposed to look like that," Chloe says. "Now watch. I want to see if Noah's playing."

I thought play was intended to be enjoyable, but these humans are hurting one another. I hear them grunting as their bodies slam together. It doesn't look like play. Yet, when one of them catches the deformed ball and runs it through a pair of posts, some of them are delighted. They caper about, raise their fists in the air and cheer.

"Guys don't *caper*, Welks."

"They appear to be capering," I say.

"That sounds wrong," Chloe says. "Look! There he is. He's so hot."

It is possible that Chloe can tell the Noah human has become heated during exercise. But I don't know how she can distinguish him from the others. Between the helmets on their heads, the padding on their bodies and the smears of mud, they're almost identical.

"It's his walk," Chloe tells me. "I recognize the way he moves."

Fascinating. "Shall we greet him?" I ask.

"No way," Chloe says. We turn around and begin jogging again, back the way we came. "I don't want him to think I'm stalking him."

"Stalking him? Is he your prey?"

Her only reply is a giggle.

Chapter Seven

Chloe's gym class is followed by instruction in mathematics. The equations under study are simple, and the human teacher reminds me of Professor Float. Its voice drones, and I pass most of that time in doze mode. I snap out of it when Chloe stands to gather her baggage. I notice our body has several problems.

"Our stomach is complaining," I say. "So is our gluteus maximus."

Chloe doesn't reply until we're amidst the throng of juveniles in the hall. Then she raises a hand to cover the lower portion of our face and whispers, "Gluteus maximus? You mean our butt?"

"I mean the large muscle we kept seated on that hard chair. Although it's feeling better now. Unlike our stomach. It wants more yogurt."

"Chloe?" I recognize the voice of the Madison human.

Chloe swivels our head toward Madison. "Hey."

"Itchy nose?" Madison asks.

"Uh, yeah." Chloe drops our hand. "Mosquito bite."

Madison wrinkles her nose. "That sucks." Then she laughs and adds, "Literally."

I fail to see why Madison laughed as she stated the obvious. Of course the mosquito sucked.

"You have *no* idea." Chloe sighs.

"Want to go to the caf for lunch?" Madison asks.

Lunch. A midday meal. Clearly, Madison *does* have an idea. An excellent idea.

"Sure," Chloe replies. Then she angles our head away from Madison and into our shoulder. "Mind cloak!" she hisses.

"But I have many questions," I protest.

She ignores me. I feel frustrated as we make our way through the crowd. Still, I do attempt the mind cloak. I'm getting so much practice at cloaking, I should soon be quite expert.

However, once we enter a large chamber that smells of *food*, I lose the cloak. Our stomach gurgles in response. It is impossible for me to ignore that. We join a line of juveniles viewing the food, which looks delightful. I would never have imagined that looking at something could be so fascinating. The food comes in all manner of shapes and sizes. There are fluffy green items, pale gooey items, round things, red things...Chloe selects a colorful triangular item and places it on a tray.

Madison chooses a pile of pale golden strips and pops one in her mouth. "Want a fry?" she asks.

Chloe nods, puts a fry in our mouth and chews. It's magnificent! Warm and crisp on the exterior, yet soft inside. I desperately want more, but we shuffle forward until we reach a human seated before a machine. Chloe opens her bag and withdraws a slip of paper. She hands it to the human. In return, he gives her a few metal discs.

We find a place at a table, and Chloe bites off the tip of the triangle. It is even *better* than the fry! As we chew, flavors explode inside our mouth. We swallow, and I anticipate the next bite. But instead Chloe reaches into her bag and removes a small box. What is wrong with her? Can't she feel how much our body wants the triangle?

"How's the pizza?" Madison asks. "Soggy as usual?"

"Actually," Chloe says, "it's pretty good."

It is! We need more! Chloe takes another bite. Ahhhh. While chewing this one, she fits a slender plastic tube into the box. We swallow the pizza, and then she sucks liquid from the tube. It's tasty too, I decide. Our body is happy about the liquid, but it's not pizza.

Several of the other humans we saw on our walk to school join us at the table. They resume their confusing chatter, but I keep my focus on the food. All too soon, the pizza is gone. I truly believe if Chloe was kind to her body, she'd give it more. Instead, she takes a round red item from her bag and bites into that. This tastes entirely different from the pizza. It requires more force from our teeth to mash it. It also seems somehow more *alive* than the pizza, and it's quite delicious. Our mouth fills with moisture as we chew, and after a few bites, it feels... cleaner? That might be right.

"Be back in a minute," Chloe tells the others.

"Are you going to the can?" Madison asks. "Do you want me to come?"

"Sure," Chloe says.

The *can* turns out to be a chamber offering wash and toilet facilities. Numerous juveniles are gathered there. Their chatter, combined with the sounds of flowing water and a hot-air machine, makes it noisy. When we enter a solitary cubicle, Chloe whispers, "You really like food, eh?"

"Our body likes it," I tell her.

"Yeah," Chloe agrees. "But the next time I'm eating, could you try to control yourself? My stomach is fine now, isn't it?"

I take a moment to consider our stomach. She's right. It has ceased complaining.

"See?" Chloe says. "All good. But I'm warning you, Welkin, it's going to start up again. In case you hadn't noticed, we have to go pee, too."

She's right. That uncomfortable pressure is building again. Truly, the body is a demanding vessel. That must go into my report to Float.

"Welks? I have English class next, then art. Then we'll go home and talk more, okay?"

"Until then—"

She finishes my sentence for me. "You'll work on the mind cloak. Or maybe doze mode again."

Chapter Eight

I manage to suppress my thoughts during English class. Chloe spends much of the time reading and writing. I regret that I didn't study the symbols for language. If I had, I'd be able to understand what our eyes are seeing and our hands are noting. It would be enlightening to share in this physical method of thought exchange. But since I can't, I find myself bored into doze mode.

Art is entirely different. The room we enter for this class is a disordered explosion of materials and colors. Some of the juvenile humans sit at tables, working on paper. Others perch on stools, spinning clumps of mud. They immerse their hands in the mud and cause it to change shape.

I would like to feel that mud, but Chloe has a different plan. She places a plain white rectangle on a stand alongside a tray. The tray is dotted with blobs of color, and she uses a thin metal tool to mix colors together. This is interesting. The blue and red merge to become purple, while the yellow and red become orange.

Once Chloe has several new shades, she picks up a brush. She dips the brush into a vibrant orange and strokes the paint onto the white rectangle. A long wavy line of orange appears. She dips the brush again, picking up a yellow, and swiftly adds this to the orange. The colors merge together, and where they meet, a third color appears.

Again and again, Chloe applies color to the rectangle. Sometimes she uses a fatter brush and swirls it through the colors. They blend into ever more shades, some light and some dark. The white disappears swiftly, and then I realize something astonishing.

Chloe is creating! She is making something altogether unique! She pauses and lays down the brush. We move into a tiny room lined with shelves.

"It's the supply closet, Welks," she whispers.

"Why are we here?" I ask. "I want to watch the creation."

"You know…" Her voice trails away, and she's quiet for a moment. Then she sighs and says, "I never thought of it quite like that. I just thought I was painting a memory of a sunrise I once saw."

"Painting a memory?" This is a stunning concept. "You're attempting to make thought *physical*?"

"I guess."

"Incredible," I say. I have a strange urge to shake our head, but rule one says I can't operate our body.

Chloe laughs softly and shakes our head for us. "Do you still think we're primitives?"

"Uh. Hmm. Maybe not so much. Universals can only share memory through thought transfer." I wonder if I'll be able to transfer my memory of Chloe. "Is this painting *exactly* like your memory?"

"Not exactly, no," she replies. "It's an abstract. More like the *feeling* of my memory."

"I understand," I say.

"Don't lie, Welkin. But tell me this. Do you still think art serves no purpose?"

I ponder that, but before I can answer, a human appears at the closet door. "Hey, Chloe," it says.

"Hey," Chloe responds. She removes a tube of paint from a shelf. "*There* it is. I need some cyan."

It turns out that cyan is a shade of blue. When Chloe feathers this color into the edges of her creation, even I can see why she needed it. I think she too is surprised by the change it makes. The yellows and oranges are suddenly glowing. Our eyes widen.

"Wow," she murmurs. "It was just an impulse."

She didn't plan for this effect? How did it happen, then?

The loud ringing that has sounded throughout the day occurs once more.

A hubbub of sound arises in the room as the humans chatter and rush to put materials away. Chloe begins cleaning her brushes. Under cover of the noise, she whispers, "Some accidents are good."

My impulse is to deny that. Accidents are not good. They are like variables in experiments. Unpredictable. But then, choosing Chloe as my host was a type of accident. I think perhaps she's right. Some accidents *are* good.

Chapter Nine

We walk most of the way back to Chloe's dwelling with the same juvenile group we walked to school with. When we part ways with them, I try to decide which question I should ask first. There are so many.

Chloe says, "Welks, I think I need some chocolate before we play Twenty Questions."

"I have far more than twenty," I tell her.

"Chocolate first, Welks. Trust me."

When we get to her dwelling and find this chocolate in the kitchen, I learn exactly what she means. We *need* the chocolate. We *really* need it. It is quite possibly even better than pizza.

We've finished our second morsel of the chocolate when brother Josh arrives. He brings several other juveniles with him. "Brownies!" Josh yells. They swarm over the precious chocolate. Seconds later, it's gone.

"They took it *all*," I say. "*All*."

"Typical," Chloe mutters.

Josh grins at us and raises a fist. "Check this out, Chloe." He pumps his arm downward. Immediately, a loud explosive sound emerges from his gluteus maximus.

"Omigod," Chloe says. "You're disgusting."

I fail to understand why Chloe finds this disgusting. I'm intrigued. I thought all purposely made human sound came from the vocal cords.

The band of juveniles hoots with laughter. "Pretty cool, eh?" Josh asks. "Wanna see me do it again?"

He doesn't wait for an answer. He pumps his fist and once more emits a sound. This time, the sound has a muffled, repetitive quality. It goes on for some time. But although I listen carefully, I can't understand a single word.

Chloe bursts into laughter, and the others join in. "Stutter fart," one of them yells.

"I'm outta here," Chloe says. As she stoops to grab her baggage from the floor, we encounter a noxious odor. Our nose wrinkles, and Chloe moves fast. "Nasty," she gasps. And we flee.

We take refuge in Chloe's sleeping chamber. I finally have a chance to ask some burning questions. We begin with Chloe very kindly explaining the nature of farts. "They're just escaping gas, Welks."

"Extraordinary," I reply. "What did Josh's fart say?"

"It said he ate the wrong food for lunch."

I ponder this. "In English?"

Chloe laughs again, and I find I greatly enjoy the sensation. It makes our body feel good all over. It's almost as good as running. When the laugh ends, Chloe says, "No, Welkin. Farts don't *say* anything. They're some sort of chemical reaction. From digesting food."

"Ahhh," I say. "Yes. I studied that. So somehow, Josh has learned the art of controlling his gas emissions?"

"I wouldn't call it an art," Chloe says. "But yeah, he has fart control."

"What about your reaction to the Noah human?" I ask. "It didn't seem like you had control of your body then."

"I can't really explain it," she says. "It just happens."

"Does he get breathless too?" I ask.

Chloe giggles. "I hope so."

She seats us at a desk and switches on an electrical device. I wonder if this will involve our hair but soon find out it's a communication tool.

"It's called a computer, Welks. I use it to talk to my friends."

"We already did that," I say. "A short time ago."

"Yeah, but we didn't *finish* talking," she says.

"When will you be finished?"

"Hmm," she says. "Probably never. Unless we have a fight."

Ah. Primitives.

"I wish you'd stop thinking that. We're *not* primitives." She clicks some buttons on the computer and says, "I'll show you."

Images appear on the screen of humans with bulging brows and sloped foreheads. Some of them have head hair extending over large areas of skin. Others carry weapons and are shown battling other beings.

"See?" Chloe taps the screen. "*Those* are primitives. We've evolved since then."

"Perhaps," I tell her. "But Universals have evolved further."

"I'm not so sure about that," she says. "You're *different*. But are you *better*?"

"We are superior," I say automatically.

"How?" she asks. "So you don't have bodies. But I think since you've been here, I like my body more than ever."

She has a point. The body is limiting, yet—

"And another thing," she says. "Humans believe in helping others. Most of us, anyway. Do Universals ever help anyone but themselves?"

"Of course we do." Don't we?

"Hmm," Chloe says. "Okay. How about you use your superior intelligence to help me with my math homework?"

I agree to do that. Chloe must state the problems aloud, as I can't read the symbols. The questions are easy. Chloe whines when I explain too quickly, but we work through it.

She is pleased. "Thanks, Welkin. I couldn't get some of this stuff, but I do now."

"Glad I could help," I tell her. And I am.

We are called then, by the mother human, to come for supper. I encounter both of Chloe's parents in the kitchen. They are like Chloe's friends, talking about people and events that aren't present. They're also similar to the adult humans in the school. They give instructions, especially to Josh. For example, they forbid farting while eating.

I place my focus on the food. It's a dish known as stir-fry—a mixture of plant matter, sauce and noodles. Each mouthful tastes different, and some morsels are better than others. It's a delight to find her parents have saved the best food for last. The mother calls it lemon pudding. Every spoonful is superb.

When the eating is done, our stomach is happy. I'm happy. It seems Chloe is not happy with the task of cleaning up the kitchen. She sighs, and we move slowly to start but soon speed up. When we're done, we join her mother in another room. There, we watch a device that emits sound and displays video. I recall that it's known as a TV and that some humans are strangely attached to it. It displays images of cavorting humans.

"They're dancing," Chloe mutters.

"Hmm?" says the mother.

"Uh…I was wondering," Chloe says. "Is it okay if I go to the dance on Friday?"

The mother squints at us. "Who are you going with?"

Chloe shrugs. "Just my friends."

"I suppose it'll be all right," the mother says. "Your father or I will pick you up when it's over."

"Great," Chloe says. "Thanks."

We continue watching the TV. Chloe and her mother appear to be fascinated, but I find it boring. I'd rather run or eat or attempt farting. I'm relieved when we depart that room to go back up the stairs.

"I need a shower," Chloe says.

This proves to be another lengthy process in body care. I enjoy the sensation of warm water washing over our skin, but tending to our body hair again is tedious. It seems Chloe must remove tiny hairs from certain places. She uses a tool to scrape hair from our legs and under our arms. Then we must deal with the head hair.

"Why not scrape that hair off too?" I ask.

"Because I like it," she says. "Don't you?"

I consider the hair. "Perhaps it helps you feel connected to your hairy ancestors?"

"Omigod," she says. "Forget it." She yawns as she puts the hair-drying device back into a cupboard. "Having you in my head is exhausting, Welks."

"It is?" I ask.

"Yeah." We return to her sleeping chamber. She switches off the light and places our body in the bed. "And for *some* reason, I didn't have the greatest sleep last night, either."

I suspect I may have had something to do with that. Me and the mosquitos.

"You got it," she mumbles. "Please tell me you can do your doze thing for the night."

"I'll try," I say. I sense her consciousness fading. It's strange how I can detect that shift yet still can't hear her thoughts.

"Welks," she murmurs. "Stop thinking."

It is peaceful, lying here. Our body is comfortable. There's nothing to see with our eyes closed, and the only sounds are quite distant. I wonder how long we'll remain like this.

"Welkin!" Chloe hisses. "Go to sleep." She shifts our body onto its side.

Doze mode, I tell myself. For a time, I succeed. But I wake during the night and don't recall where I am. I feel trapped, and it's frightening. My impulse is to think myself *elsewhere*, but something resists. I'm held back—and then I remember I'm inside a human host. Somehow it has become a part of me. Or I've become part of it. Our separation at the end of bioethics class will be difficult.

"Difficult," Chloe murmurs.

Chapter Ten

The next day with Chloe is much like the first. We care for the body, eat and attend school. I look forward to returning to her dwelling, where we can speak freely. When we finally separate from her friends, I ask, "Can we run for the remainder of the journey?"

But we stop abruptly. "Aww, look!" Chloe says. "A kitten."

We observe a small furry being lurking under a shrub. Chloe swerves off the cement path we are following and crouches down beside it. "Hi, kitty," she coos.

"Does it speak English too?" I ask.

"Not exactly," Chloe says. "But it can learn some words. And it knows it's a kitty." She stretches out our hand to stroke the being. "Don't you, kitty?"

Kitty reacts by arching its back and emitting a rumbling sound.

"See? It's purring. Oh"—her voice goes high—"you are too cute."

Contact with the kitty is pleasing. Its hair is soft, and our palm senses the vibration of its sound. There is something more. As it responds by returning the pressure of our touch, we can feel its life energy. "Do you

think I might try operating our hand?"
I ask.

"No. Well, maybe. But just for a
minute. You have to be very careful.
Kittens are delicate."

She allows our hand to go limp,
and I concentrate hard. I tell the nerves
and the muscles of the hand to move.
At first, nothing happens. Then all at
once, it twitches. I did it! I turn it one
way and then the other. It's a fascinating
mechanism.

"This is totally weird," Chloe
mutters.

I'd like to master the operation of
the hand before placing it on the kitty.
I decide to test my control of the fingers.
I move one, then another. Then I wiggle
them all at once, and the kitten pounces.

It wraps all four legs around our
hand and begins to bite. Its teeth are
sharp. As if that weren't enough, it flat-
tens its ears and begins kicking with

its hind feet. Its feet are armored with pointed claws. I'm so shocked that I abandon control of the hand.

Chloe laughs as she uses our other hand to gently detach the wicked creature.

"It's not wicked, Welkin," she says. "It's playing."

"It attacked us," I point out.

"You asked for it. Kittens can't resist wiggling things." Chloe holds out our bitten hand and says, "Look. It didn't even draw blood. We're fine."

She stands and cuddles the beast to our torso. It purrs more loudly than ever. "We really *can* feel its life, can't we?" she marvels. "I mean, I remember when my friend's guinea pig died. When I touched it, it felt so strange, like it was empty."

"Its energy had departed," I say.

"Yeah. I guess." She gazes about. "I wonder where this kitten came from."

"My guess would be from a mother cat," I say sourly. My first opportunity to operate our body ruined by a miniature savage!

"Don't sulk, Welks. Obviously, it came from a mother cat. What I meant was, I wonder where it belongs?"

"Under that shrub," I say.

"That's not safe. We can't leave it there." Chloe looks at the nearest dwelling. "I'd like to take it home with me, but…" She sighs. We carry the kitten across a grassy area and up to a door. She pushes a button on the wall, and we hear a chime sound within. Seconds later, we hear footsteps approaching, and the door swings open.

"Hi," Chloe says. "I found this kitten out by the street and I was wondering—"

"Fang!" the human shrieks. "How did you get out there?" It reaches for the kitten.

Our body is reluctant to hand the kitten over, but we do. "Fang sure is cute," Chloe says.

"Cute, and a whole lot of trouble," the human replies. But it does the same odd thing Chloe did, raising its voice as it says, "Aren't you, Fangsy-wangsy? You're a nuisance, yes you are." Fang embeds its teeth in the human's hand. I find this oddly pleasing.

"Okay, then," Chloe says. "I guess we'd better get going."

The human squints at us and then looks past our shoulder. "We?" it asks.

"Oh. Ha ha. I mean, *me*. Better go. Bye." We turn and scurry back across the grass.

Once we're back on the path, Chloe says, "This is getting to me, Welks."

"What do you mean?" I ask.

"I mean you being in my head. Me saying *we* to that lady. It's weird."

"How so?" I ask.

She's quiet for a moment. "It just is. I'm glad at least my thoughts are private."

I am *not* glad about that. But then, I recall the many times when I was unable to cloak my thoughts from others. Privacy of the mind is an incomparable freedom.

"So then you get it, Welks," Chloe murmurs.

She spends the remainder of the day avoiding me. She does this by staying around other humans. We play something known as a video game with Josh. We watch TV with the mother. We chat at length with her friends, both via computer and telephone.

When the time to sleep arrives, she surprises me by asking, "Why do you have feelings, Welks?"

"Feelings?"

"As in, emotions. I know you have them. But," she adds, "all you can *do* is think."

"Thinking is a powerful force," I tell her. "Thoughts are a form of energy. They can influence other energies. Our Thought Archives are an excellent example of this."

"What are Thought Archives?" she asks.

"They are an energy field where we Universals can store and share knowledge from our minds."

"Huh," Chloe says. "Sounds sort of like the 'cloud' we humans have in cyberspace."

Before I can fully consider this, she asks, "But what about emotions?"

"Universals have debated the value of emotions for as long as we've existed. Some say we should discard them, since they are not logical. Others say emotions enrich the experience of life."

She rolls our eyes. "What do *you* say?"

"I haven't decided."

Chloe sighs. "Okay. Good night, Welkin."

By morning, Chloe is lively again. "It's your last day, Welks. Any requests for a new physical experience?"

"Hmm. I have observed humans being transported via machines and I've wondered—"

"No problem," she says. "We're taking the bus to the mall after school. I want to get a new top for the dance."

The transport experience is disappointing. I find it doesn't utilize the body in any unique manner. We simply seat ourselves in a rectangular chamber and lurch along until we reach the mall. This is a massive structure, holding many objects, where humans wander aimlessly. Chloe is not among the aimless. She finds clothing displays and hunts among them with great purpose.

I pass the return journey by estimating the percentage of human time required to care for the physical form. Feeding, sleeping, washing and decorating the body takes almost half their time. Moving the body from place to place takes more time. Then there's time spent preparing food and cleaning the tools used for that. I'm still working on my calculations when we reach Chloe's bedchamber.

"Don't forget washing clothes and cleaning house," she says. "We have to do that to prevent stinking and germs. Plus, when we're adults, there's more. We have to work so we have money to buy the food and shelter for our bodies. Also clothes."

She pulls her new clothing item from a bag. "I love this new top."

We look at the top. I see pink fabric designed to fit our torso. It's similar to other clothing items Chloe owns. I fail to understand why she wanted to obtain it.

Chloe places the new top on her bed. "It's sort of like art, Welkin. I'm trying to create a new image of me. For the dance. About that..." She stops.

"Yes?" I prompt.

"I was wondering..." She stops again.

"About what?" I ask.

"Um. Okay. Well, first, I want to ask you something. What do Universals do for fun?"

"We think," I say.

"Thinking is *fun*?" Chloe asks.

"Sometimes. It depends on *what* we're thinking."

"I don't get it," she says.

"It's not complicated. You think too. Haven't you noticed that some of your thoughts bring you joy?"

"Yeah," she says slowly. "But they can also make me sad. And really, it's not my thoughts that do that. It's the things my thoughts are *about*."

"But you can decide what to think about. You control your thoughts, don't you?" I ask.

"Um. Not exactly, Welks. They just *happen*. Yours do too. I can hear them, remember?"

She has me there. "I must admit, being trapped in a body makes it more difficult to control thought. But it's not impossible. Some members of your species have understood this for thousands of years. For example, Marcus Aurelius said, *Your life is what your thoughts make it.*"

"Hmm," Chloe says. "Guess I'll have to *think* about that. But I want to ask you. I mean, I'll bet you're tired of being trapped in a body, right? So maybe you might want to, uh, leave class a little early?"

"What do you mean?" I ask.

"Aw, Welkin. I don't want you to take this the wrong way. It's actually been pretty cool having you here. But it's hard sometimes too. And I really like Noah, right? I was thinking about the dance tonight, and it's just," she finishes in a rush, "I'd like you to leave before the dance."

"I don't understand."

"Hearing you thinking all those things about my body being electrified around him is distracting. And weird. So," she takes a deep breath, "I'd like to go to the dance without you."

She isn't making sense. Either we go to the dance together or neither of us goes. She can't very well go dancing when her body is—

"Dead?" Chloe's voice is faint. "I'm going to die?" Our body sags to the floor. Our heart is pounding in our chest, and I hear our blood rushing. "No. No, no. *No*."

"Obviously," I say. "All host bodies die."

Chapter Eleven

Chloe doesn't speak again for some time. When she finally does, she asks, "Why didn't you tell me?"

"I thought you knew. You hear my thoughts. Although perhaps I haven't thought about this since the mosquito."

"You should have *told* me," she wails. "I'd *never* have let you stay if I'd known."

Before I can respond, she continues. Her voice is brittle as she says, "Only I guess that wouldn't have made any difference. By the time I knew you were here, it was already too late, wasn't it?"

Salt water begins seeping from our eyes. It stings.

"I hate you," Chloe says.

I find this surprising. "Why?"

"Why? *Why?*" Her voice rises shrilly. "You're going to kill me, and you think I should be fine with that?"

Our body convulses with sobs.

"It's *not*," Chloe gasps between sobs, "not *our* body! It's *mine*."

"But it's only a body," I say. "I'm not killing *you*, Chloe. Only this body will die."

"You're crazy!" she shrieks. "If my body dies, *I* die."

"Don't be ridiculous," I tell her. "Your life energy will simply move on. Perhaps to another body or—"

"I don't want another body. I want *this* one. I like it here. I *am* my body. Or it's me. Whatever. You're evil, Welkin. Evil!"

I find myself remembering Professor Float's instructions. He did stress the importance of suppressing the host. Had I gained control in the first place, I wouldn't have to deal with this hysterical reaction. "Chloe." I make myself speak slowly as I point out the obvious. "Your body will die soon anyway. It will grow old and cease being operational."

"No," she says. "Not for a long time. A lifetime. *My* lifetime. I want my life, Welkin. I want it here." She pats our chest. "Right here. In this body I was born with."

"But—"

"I have *dreams*, Welkin. I want to travel the world. Climb mountains. Run races. Ride a bike and ride in cars and on boats and trains and airplanes and…

and *horses*. I want to get my own kitten and swim in the ocean. Visit the Louvre in Paris. And fall in *love* with someone who loves me back."

I try again. "But—"

"No! I need more time with the people I love right here and now. My friends and family. If what you say is true about life energy going into bodies, then mine must have come into *this* one for a reason. I'm supposed to be *here*. I'm supposed to have *this* life."

She may have a point.

"An *excellent* point, Welks. You have no right to take this life away from me. There must be *some* way you can leave without killing me."

There is no way. When my energy entered her body, it bound itself to hers. It's a process that I don't fully understand. Energy, especially life energy, is a mystery even to Universals.

"Then," Chloe says sadly, "there's only one solution, Welkin."

For once, I know what she's thinking. "You want me to stay with you until…?"

"Until the end. I don't *want* that, Welks. But if it comes down to a choice between dying now or having you share my whole life," She shudders, then draws a deep breath. "I choose to live."

I'd fail bioethics class. Again. But at least I'd have a short break before having to repeat it. Again. Still, the thought of being stuck inside the confines of this body is depressing. "Are you *certain* you want to stay here?" I ask.

"Absolutely," Chloe says.

"It's a difficult choice," I say.

"Do you remember when you started telling me about time, Welkin? Just now I heard you thinking my lifetime would be a short break for you. So I'm wondering. How long do Universals live?"

"How long? I don't know. I've never known one to stop existing."

"You live *forever*?" she asks.

"Forever is a peculiar concept. Very difficult to grasp. And time flows differently in my dimension. In human time, I estimate I came into being when those pyramid tombs on Earth were built." I pause before adding, "And I'm still a juvenile."

"Welkin! You're ancient." Chloe shakes our head. "So my lifetime compared to yours is super short?"

"Yes. I can guess why you're asking about that. If I stayed for your human life, it wouldn't take much of my time." I don't say it, but there are other factors to consider. For one, there *could* be a reason her life energy belongs in this body. It *could* have a purpose here.

Going further, part of that purpose could be the effect it has on other lives. No life exists without affecting others. And finally, as primitive as she is, I've come to care for Chloe.

"So you'll do it? Omigod! Thank you, Welks!" She springs to our feet and twirls us around.

"Stop that," I tell her. "You're making us dizzy."

She stops abruptly. "Sorry. If you stay, I'll try to stop being so bossy. With my—with *our* body."

That doesn't sound like Chloe.

"I know," she quavers. "But if you don't like what I'm doing, you could just...*phhtt*. Go."

"Chloe," I say, "if I stay so you can finish your life here, will it truly be yours if you live in fear of me leaving?"

"I'm not ready to die," she says. "So I'll have to try to keep you happy."

That seems wrong. This situation has become complicated. "I must ponder the variables, Chloe."

She sighs so deeply that our entire body trembles. We slowly sink down onto the bed. Once again, she passes considerable time in silence. Eventually, she says, "Okay, Welks. You know how I feel. I want to live. I'm going to count on you agreeing that this is the right choice. So," she says as she stands, "we're going to the dance."

Chapter Twelve

The dance is located in the large chamber where we met the Dork-Doran. It has been transformed. It reminds me of the time I accidentally entered a gas being.

Chloe crouches to adjust a strap on our shoe. "A *gas* being, Welks?" She doesn't have to worry about other humans overhearing her. The sound in the room is thunderous.

"Yes," I tell her. "I was studying chemistry, and the teacher wanted us to experience an explosion. The gas being was in a star going nova. It was barely sentient, yet it was capable of perceiving light. It allowed me to glimpse flashing bursts much like these here, which—"

"Okay, okay. I get it. For a minute I thought you meant someone like Josh. You can tell me the rest later. I want to dance now." Chloe stands and steps close to Madison. She must yell to ask, "Have you seen Noah?"

"Not yet," Madison yells back.

For a fraction of a moment, the noise ceases. It starts again, and Chloe yells, "Oh, I *love* this song. Let's go!"

We had been standing on the fringe of the writhing crowd, but now we plunge right in. I'm rather frightened. The juveniles appear to have lost control of their limbs. Also, having viewed the cavorting humans on TV, I fear dancing will hurt our body. Those humans moved in extraordinary ways.

I hear Chloe laugh, and I realize it's a beautiful sound. Then all at once we are jiggling about. Our feet shift back and forth and up and down, and our arms flail the air. Our torso and our gluteus maximus bob from side to side, and our head hair swishes wildly. Chloe does nothing to contain it. This makes me fear she's gone insane.

But then I notice there's a relationship between our movements and the sound. I pay close attention, and sure enough, our motions follow the music. We are harmonizing with it. Amazing!

We dance through several more songs. The more we do it, the more I like it. The music surrounds us and goes through us too. I can actually feel some of the low-range thumps reverberating in our stomach. It's like running in that I feel myself becoming one with the body. Thoughts pale when the body is in action.

But we're not entirely unaware. No. We notice at once when Noah dances into view. Our body notices too. It suffers that strange electrical current, and Chloe has our face smiling so widely that our cheeks feel strained.

"Hey," she yells.

"Hey," Noah yells back.

We continue dancing. Only now we watch Noah and smile while he does the same. This goes on for a while, all of us bobbing with the music. Multicolored lights flash over us, pulsing in time with the stomach-felt beat. I note that sometimes Noah appears to be green, sometimes orange or blue. Occasionally, he's stricken with an intense clear beam that washes all the color away. That has the effect of making his head look like a skull. I wonder if the lights have the same effect on our appearance.

"Gah." Chloe chokes.

"What?" Noah yells.

"Nothing," Chloe yells back.

The tempo of the music changes. It slows, and our movement slows with it. We glance about and see some of the juveniles departing. Others begin forming linked pairs. For a fraction of a moment, our body tenses as if we're preparing to flee. Then Noah looms close and places his hands on the midsection of our torso.

We experience another jolt of electricity. Then we take a quick breath and place our hands on his shoulders. And, just as when we touched the kitten, our hands sense his life energy. We smile. He smiles. We shuffle our feet from side to side in such a way that we go nowhere.

"How's it goin'?" Noah asks.

Chloe giggles. I fail to see why. "Good," she replies. "How's it goin' with you?"

"Good," he says.

We all smile some more.

"Still talking to yourself?" Noah asks.

Ever so slightly, our muscles stiffen. "Um," Chloe says, "actually, I don't really—" She stops. Interesting. I wonder if she was about to tell him about me. I wonder if she'll ever tell anyone about me.

Then all at once Noah staggers. If it weren't for our grabbing hold of his arm, I think he may have fallen. He steadies himself and says, "Hello, Welkin."

We gasp.

"Please, act naturally," Noah says. "Carry on dancing."

But we don't carry on dancing. We come to a full stop. Our mouth gapes open, and we stare at him. "What the…" Chloe begins.

"Professor Float," I say. I'd recognize that flat tone anywhere. "You're here. Or rather, you're *there*. In Noah's body."

"Indeed," Float says. "It's most convenient."

This can only mean one thing. For Chloe's sake, I can't bring myself to say it aloud. But she manages to squeak, "Are you here for Welkin?"

"Of course," Float replies. "Time's up. Welkin must return to our dimension and provide his report."

Chapter Thirteen

Our body feels strangely numb and stands frozen in place.

"Continue moving," Float instructs. "We don't want to attract undue attention." Noah's feet shuffle from side to side, but they're no longer in time with the music.

Chloe manages to move our feet once or twice, but then she halts again.

"Don't you think my *dying* on the dance floor will attract attention?" she asks.

"I am certain that it will," Float says. "But we won't see that happen."

"No." Chloe's voice is ragged. "You'll be gone by then."

In that moment, I know what I must do. "Professor Float? I'm not returning to our dimension yet. I understand I'll fail your class again, but I've decided to stay with Chloe."

"Don't be foolish, Welkin," Float says. "Why would you do a thing like that?"

"Because it wouldn't be right. It would be wrong of me to cut her life short."

"Is that so?" Float asks. "Tell me, Welkin, why do you believe this?"

"Because we think maybe she's here for a reason," I tell him.

"Hmm." Float tilts Noah's head. "What reason might that be?"

"We don't know yet," Chloe answers.

"That's a lot of maybe and don't know," Float says. "Welkin, surely you can state your case more clearly. Allow me to give you a hint. What does *bioethics* mean?"

"Erm," I say. "Well. The *bio* part is for biology. That's the scientific study of life and living matter. The *ethics* part is the study of what is morally right or wrong."

"Exactly." Float nods Noah's head.

"Omigod," Chloe cries. "I just realized! You're going to kill Noah too!"

From the corner of our eye, I notice some of the other juveniles glancing our way. They may not be able to hear what's being said over the music, but they seem to sense that something is amiss.

"Calm yourself, human," Float says. "Nobody is going to be killed."

"Killing our bodies is as good as killing *us*," Chloe replies. "At least the 'us' me and Noah are meant to be."

"I'm not here to debate that with you," Float tells her. "I'm here to test Welkin. I want to know if Welkin can correctly state a reason for choosing to remain with you. Can you, Welkin?"

I know why Float made me define *bioethics*. I even know the answer to the question. But putting it into words is difficult. "Um," I begin. "Okay. In your class, Professor, we are learning the correct way to study life. I'd say that means we must show respect for what life truly *is*. Which is a mystery. So it would be wrong for me to interfere with Chloe's life."

"Ah," Float says. "Now we're getting somewhere. Excellent. But answer me this. If you stay in her body, won't that also interfere with her present life?"

"Not as much as it would if he leaves," Chloe chimes in.

"Indeed." Noah's mouth smiles. Float is quite expert at operating a human body. "So I'd say you have a dilemma, Welkin. Obviously, your choice to enter a host was made without thinking through the consequences."

"But," I sputter, "that was the *assignment*! You made me do it."

"Did I?" Float asks. "I *forced* you to do this?"

Such an annoying question. Of course he didn't force me. I chose this project of my own stupid free will. "I only wanted to pass bioethics," I whine.

"My congratulations," Float says. "You've passed. And now we must go."

"But—" Chloe and I speak as one.

Float cuts us off. "No buts. Welkin, passing basic bioethics means you're ready to begin advanced bioethics."

I'm stunned. "Advanced bioethics? Me?"

"Yes. Class starts now. Your first lesson is in body-save withdrawal. It requires the trust and cooperation of your host. I believe she may give you that."

"Are you saying—" I begin.

"That Welkin can go—" Chloe continues.

"Without killing her body?" I finish.

"Precisely," Float answers.

Chloe chortles with delight and twirls both us and Noah-Float. When she's done, I want to give our head a shake, and Chloe does this for me.

"Professor Float, why didn't you tell me this was possible *before*?" I ask.

"You don't always pay attention to the things I say, Welkin."

I can't deny that.

"And," Float continues, "some things are better learned through experience. I find that students who face this choice personally gain deeper understanding."

"So what do we have to do?" Chloe asks. "Do we need to go stand in a field or something? So Welkin can beam out?"

"No, no. We can remain right here. It's quite simple, really."

The notes of the slow-tempo song are beginning to fade. Some of the couples dancing nearby begin to separate. "Quickly now," Float says. "I must assist Welkin on his first attempt. For that, we require close contact."

"Closer than this?" I ask.

"Chloe must connect a breath portal."

"Huh?" Chloe asks.

"Connect your nostril or mouth to a similar portal on this Noah body," Float instructs. "I believe such behavior is common in you humans."

"Uh," Chloe says, "you must mean kissing." She takes a deep breath. Then she places our mouth on Noah's.

It feels strange there. Awkward. And yet it's interesting too. I didn't realize our lips had so many sensitive nerves.

But before I can analyze it further, Float's life energy finds mine. The contact is similar to the electrical current I experienced in Chloe's body. But Float's energy isn't running about wildly. It is focused, and it begins pulling me into Noah's mouth. And out again, through a Noah nostril.

"Gently, now," Float says. "Gather only yourself. Take no part of the human."

Take no part of Chloe. That's easier said than done. I've inhabited her body right down to the molecules. It's as if my energy is water that I poured into a Chloe glass of water. And the water has mixed to become one.

Still, bit by bit, I find myself. Slowly at first, then faster and faster.

"Good, good. That's it." Float encourages me. "I'm free of the Noah skin bag. He's becoming self-aware again.

Hopefully, he'll cooperate with maintaining contact."

For the first time since I entered her body, I hear Chloe's thoughts. "He'd *better* keep kissing me."

I'm almost out. Enough to hear Noah's thoughts now too. "Whoa! What the...?" He draws his mouth away from Chloe's, and I hang between them. But only for a second, because Chloe's mouth reconnects, and he thinks, "I thought she was *shy?*"

Obviously, he doesn't know Chloe very well. Shy? Hardly. "She's amazing," I tell him.

I think he actually hears me. His next thought is exactly that. *She's amazing.*

Then, I'm free and clear.

Float says, "Think *home*, Welkin. I'll see you there." And Float is gone.

Home, I think. But I don't want to go. *Home, home.* I *really* don't want to go there. I want to experience all the things Chloe mentioned. Swim in an ocean, climb a mountain, run races...

I can no longer see Chloe as I did through her eyes. I simply perceive her as a field of energy. As she separates from Noah, she thinks, "Phew!"

Does she mean *Phew! I got rid of Welkin?* Probably.

"No, Welkin," Chloe thinks. "It means I'm glad this worked."

I'm astonished. "You can still hear me?"

"Yeah. Pretty cool, huh?"

"I didn't know such a thing was possible!"

"Can you wait a minute?" she asks. Her next thoughts are less clear to me. I believe she tells Noah she'll be back soon, but her thinking is mixed with a range of emotions. Emotion does not translate precisely into thought. This is why some Universals say we should attempt to overcome it.

"Have you made up your mind about that, Welkin?" Chloe asks. "Because *I* think your emotions saved my life."

I believe she is correct.

"I know I am." Once again, her thoughts fog with emotion. "I can't believe I'm saying this, but I'm going to miss you, Welks."

"I'll miss you too, Chloe. I'm most grateful for all your help."

"Aw, that's okay." Her thoughts shift rapidly for a moment, and then she asks, "Do you remember when you said that if I let you stay, I could study you while you studied me?"

"Yes."

"Well, I think maybe I learned more about myself than I did about you."

"Is that good?" I ask.

"Oh, yeah. Really good. So thank you."

If I still inhabited her body, I believe I would feel it smiling.

"You would," Chloe says. "And Welkin?"

"Yes?"

"Do you think you might come back and visit sometime? Like maybe when you finish school?"

"Universals," I say, "never finish school."

"Wow. Really? What about that Float dude? Dudette. Whatever. Isn't that your teacher?"

"Yes, Float is a teacher. We're all teachers when we know enough about something. But we all keep learning too."

"I see," Chloe says.

"Don't lie," I reply.

"Okay, so forget that. Just visit me *soon*. As in, before I'm dead."

"I'd like that." I really would.

"Only," she says, "you can't barge into my body again."

"But—" I begin.

"No *buts*!"

If I could sigh, I would.

I sense laughter mixed with her next thought. "Being human is fabulous, right?"

It is. It really is.

Float instructed me to take no part of the human with me, but I do. I take memories. I take experiences. I take understanding. I include much of this in my final report. I note Chloe's difficulties with head hair. The mechanics of running and dancing. The necessity of eating food. The audio nature of farting.

But some things cannot be stored in the Thought Archives. Some things are un-thought. Like making memory physical in shades of color. Or losing thought when the body is at play. Or the sensation of touching another being's

life energy. Try as I might to transmit the essence of certain experiences, I can't.
Some things cannot be downloaded.

Acknowledgments

Gratitude to the ever-supportive imagineers Shelley Hrdlitschka and Diane Tullson. I deeply appreciate their belief that even my wackiest ideas can be realized on the page. My thanks also to Melanie Jeffs, superb Orca editor, and to all at Orca Book Publishers for bringing my tenth novel into being.